MW01590821

Original title:
Pearly Vales Along the Witch Hemp

Copyright © 2025 Swan Charm
All rights reserved.

Author: Kaido Väinamäe
ISBN HARDBACK: 978-1-80563-492-8
ISBN PAPERBACK: 978-1-80565-013-3

Guardian Shadows of the Timeless Woodland

In the heart of the woods where the old trees lie,
Whispers of magic in the branches sigh.
Leaves glimmer softly in the dappled light,
Guardians tread softly, veiled in the night.

Moss carpets the ground, a green velvet spread,
Footfalls of creatures, the stories they've wed.
A rhythm of secrets that echo the past,
In shadows, they dance, both solemn and vast.

The moon casts its gaze through the canopy high,
Illuminating paths where the lost spirits lie.
Each twist of the trail holds a memory spun,
Of laughter and tears that once brightly shone.

Among ancient oaks, their eyes never close,
The guardians linger, as time softly flows.
With hearts intertwined in the essence of space,
They cradle the woods, a dear, timeless place.

So roam through the twilight, where enchantments weave,

And listen for tales in the whispers of leaves.
For the shadows that guard this enchanted domain,
Are echoes of love that forever remain.

Radiance Amidst Fern-clad Mysticism

In twilight's hush, the shadows dance,
Amidst the ferns, a whispered chance.
A glow of light, so soft and rare,
Invites the heart to linger there.

Beneath the trees, where secrets weave,
The air is thick with dreams we believe.
Each leaf a story, each breath a sigh,
As starlit wonders grace the sky.

In glimmers caught between the night,
A world awakens, pure delight.
With every step, the whispers rise,
A symphony of ancient ties.

The moonlit path, a guide so wise,
Reflects the magic in our eyes.
Together, we find courage bold,
In ferns of green, our tales unfold.

As we depart, the echoes stay,
A promise made, not lost in gray.
In mystic realms, we found our way,
Forever bound in twilight's play.

Glimmers of the Unknown in the Mystic Glade

In the glade where shadows play,
Glimmers beckon, leading stray.
A soft mist hangs, enchantments swirl,
Lost dreams in each leaf unfurl.

Through ancient trees, the moonlight creeps,
Secrets whispered, silence keeps.
Find the path beyond the veil,
Where time flows like a gentle trail.

Soft melodies on breezes ride,
Calling hearts that dare collide.
In every echo, a story waits,
Unlocking bounds, defying fates.

The air hums low with potent lore,
Each step taken opens more.
With every breath, a spark ignites,
In the glade, true magic bites.

So wander forth, embrace the light,
For in this realm, dreams take flight.
In glimmers found, forever true,
The unknown whispers just for you.

Embered Paths of Wanderlust and Wonder

Beneath the boughs where embers gleam,
With every step, we chase a dream.
Paths entwined with flickering fire,
Lead the heart to deep desire.

The night unfolds, a cloak of stars,
Inviting souls to journey far.
Each crackling spark a tale to tell,
Of wanderlust, where tempests swell.

In whispered winds, adventures stir,
Each heartbeat echoes with a blur.
Footsteps echo on the earth,
Revealing wonders, rebirth.

Through forest dark and shadows bright,
With every glance, we find the light.
Together we roam, hand in hand,
Exploring where the heart has planned.

So follow close the trails we create,
As embers guide and dreams await.
In paths of wonder, we'll find our way,
Forever bound to roam and play.

Echoes of Enchantment within the Secret Grove

In the grove where silence sings,
Echoes dance on gentle wings.
With every rustle, secrets breathe,
In this haven, we've believed.

Shadows stretch in twilight's glow,
As whispers chase the sun's warm flow.
The rhythm of the leaves enthralls,
Each sigh a tale the forest calls.

The heart attunes to nature's grace,
In every nook, a hidden place.
With laughter ringing, spirits rise,
In this enchanted paradise.

A tapestry of light and shade,
Each step a memory we've made.
In every echo, magic dwells,
In secret grove, where wonder swells.

So linger long, let moments stay,
In this embrace, we find our way.
For in the whispers, truth does prove,
Our souls unite in this great grove.

Hues of Mystery in Moon-Kissed Flora

Under the silver glow, shadows dance,
Whispers of night in a spectral trance.
Petals unfurl, secrets unfold,
Painting the world in stories untold.

Frosted dew clings, a ghostly embrace,
Mirroring dreams in a delicate lace.
Colors converge in a mystical hue,
Holding the whispers of long-lost dew.

Celestial Reflections on Serene Meadows

Stars wink gently in twilight's clasp,
Soft breezes carry night's velvet rasp.
Silhouettes linger where daisies sway,
Guardians of secrets at end of day.

The moonlight weaves a silver thread,
'Twixt blades of grass where silence is spread.
Each shimmering glimmer, a tale to be told,
Of laughter and shadows, of brave and bold.

Tapestry of Secrets in the Shimmering Thicket

In the heart of the thicket, stories entwine,
Rustling leaves weave a pattern divine.
Muffled whispers float through the air,
Each a connection, a silent prayer.

Twinkling lights in the thicket invite,
Each flicker a moment, a fragment of night.
The trees hold their secrets, ancient and wise,
Beneath their gnarled boughs, the past softly lies.

Enigma Weaved in Twilight's Waters

Rippling waters mimic a lover's sigh,
Reflecting whispers as the stars float by.
Cool hands of twilight trace every wave,
A ballet of memories, the restless brave.

In shadows below, the silence hums low,
Each ripple a tale where wishes can flow.
Twilight's embrace, a shroud gently cast,
Holding the magic of moments amassed.

Magic Sown in the Secret Clearing

In the hush of the evening's glow,
Glistening dew, a soft tableau.
Whispers of spells in the gentle breeze,
Nature's heart beats, a tune that frees.

Misty shadows dance with grace,
Elfin laughter, a hidden place.
Charmed petals flutter, wild and bright,
Guardians of secrets in the falling night.

A flicker of light from a wand unseen,
Enchanted trust where the magic's been.
Each sparkling mote tells a tale anew,
In the secret clearing, dreams come true.

Reveries Beneath the Treetops

Underneath the boughs so wide,
Thoughts unfurl like a gentle tide.
Sunlight dances through leafy lace,
A tapestry woven with time and space.

Quiet moments bring peace to the mind,
In shadows where wonders intertwine.
Curious creatures peek and play,
As harmony lingers throughout the day.

Whispers of wishes ride on the air,
Stories of love and timeless care.
Beneath the treetops, hearts find wings,
In reveries deep, where magic sings.

Serene Whispers of the Arcane Land

In the twilight, soft and solemn,
Ancient echoes in darkened volume.
Mysterious paths twine through the night,
Leading the lost to enchanted light.

A brook babbles soft, a gentle muse,
Carrying tales of the wise and the profuse.
Leaves murmur secrets, wisdom shared,
The guardian spirits, tenderly cared.

Stars flicker softly, a blanket of dreams,
A dance of the cosmos in silver beams.
Each whisper holds magic, pure and grand,
In the serene heart of the arcane land.

Nostalgia of the Hidden Grove

In the grove where memories intertwine,
Echoes of laughter through ages shine.
Time weaves stories in branches above,
A tapestry stitched with threads of love.

Faded shadows of youth appear,
Moments of joy, mingled with fear.
Sunlight dapples the ground in gold,
While whispers of dreams softly unfold.

The scent of wildflowers drifts on air,
Sending hearts back to places rare.
In the hidden grove, nostalgia flows,
With each gentle breeze, a memory grows.

Harmonies of Nature in the Dreamweavers' Vale

In the vale where whispers sing,
The trees are draped in silver light.
Blossoms twirl in gentle spring,
Awakening dreams that take flight.

Crickets strum their twilight song,
While fireflies dance in scattered grace.
The river flows, a melody strong,
As the night embraces each trace.

Moonlit paths of woven beams,
Guide the wanderers with delight.
Nature hums her ancient themes,
Entwining day and starry night.

Breezes carry the secrets bold,
Of creatures hid in leafy bower.
In the vale, a tale unfolds,
Of dreams awakened with each hour.

Here, the heart finds sweet repose,
In harmony with every sound.
In the vale where magic grows,
A symphony of life is found.

Bewitched Meadows of Iridescent Twilight

In meadows lush with hues so bright,
Beneath the sun's last golden ray,
The flowers spark with pure delight,
As daylight gives its slow ballet.

Dancing shadows sway and glide,
As dusk unfolds her silken shawl.
A world where every heart can bide,
In twilight's captivating thrall.

Whispers weave through emerald grass,
Where wildlings frolic, free and sly.
Each moment's charm, a fleeting pass,
Carried forth on the evening sigh.

Stars awaken, glittering high,
As the moon spills silver on the field.
In this bewitchment, we rely,
On the magic twilight has revealed.

Here in the meadows, lost in trance,
Nature's splendor will confide.
In the twilight's daring dance,
The mysteries of night abide.

Celestial Tune of the Hyacinth Glade

In the glade where hyacinths bloom,
The air is thick with fragrant dreams.
Gentle notes dispel the gloom,
As sunlight pours in golden streams.

Butterflies weave through petals bright,
Each flutter a secret ballet.
In this garden of pure delight,
Nature whispers what words cannot say.

Crickets chant their rhythmic cheer,
While shadows creep in crescent light.
Every moment, crystal clear,
As day yields once more to night.

Moonlit glances awaken souls,
To dance at edges, wild and free.
In the harmony of nature's roles,
Hearts align in perfect glee.

In hyacinth's embrace, we stand,
Listening to the starry tune.
In this glade, with open hand,
We find solace beneath the moon.

The Dusk's Embrace in the Haunting Grove

In the grove where shadows creep,
Mysteries stir with gentle sigh.
Beneath the trees, the secrets sleep,
While echoes of the night drift by.

Cloaked in twilight, whispers flow,
As stars ignite the inky sky.
The haunting breeze begins to blow,
Carrying tales of days gone by.

Moonlight glimmers on the stream,
Where dreams converge upon the shore.
In this space, we weave a dream,
Of stories lost, but wanting more.

Each rustle leaves a trace of lore,
In haunted spaces, old and wise.
The dusk enchants forevermore,
As time slips softly 'neath the skies.

In the grove, we find our place,
Where dusk's embrace keeps shadows near.
In this haunting, gentle space,
The essence of the night, so dear.

Fragile Moments in the Luminous Glen

In the glen where shadows play,
Each leaf a whisper of the day.
Softly glows the twilight sun,
A fleeting moment, swiftly spun.

Crimson blooms by silver streams,
Dreams entwined within their seams.
Gentle breezes carry light,
Through the whispers of the night.

Beneath the stars, a magic spark,
Songs of hope ignite the dark.
Every step, a tale to weave,
In this realm, we dare believe.

Time eludes with every sigh,
Fragile moments flutter by.
In the glen where heartbeats pause,
We find solace in the cause.

So let us dwell, not rush away,
In luminous glens, where dreams can stay.
With every glance, a story shared,
In the fragile space, we cared.

Dance of the Phoenix within the Timeless Thicket

In the thicket, shadows twirl,
A fiery dance, a vibrant swirl.
The phoenix rises, bold and free,
In a world of endless mystery.

With feathers gleaming, bright as dawn,
It spins and twirls upon the lawn.
Each flap a promise of rebirth,
A tale of courage, woven worth.

In timeless thickets, wild and vast,
The echoes of the past hold fast.
Every flame ignites the air,
A reminder of the love we share.

The music calls, a haunting sound,
In every heartbeat, magic found.
Together we shall make our stand,
As one, we weave through life's strand.

Embers glow in deep twilight,
A dance of hope ignites the night.
Within this thicket, wild and grand,
A phoenix rises, hand in hand.

Flourish of Wishes in the Enchanted Wood

In enchanted woods where secrets breathe,
A chorus sings, the wishes wreathe.
Each fluttered leaf, a dream unfurls,
A tapestry of hidden pearls.

Amongst the trees, where shadows dwell,
A gentle magic casts its spell.
With every step, a wish ignites,
As starlit paths embrace the nights.

Softly glows the moonlit way,
Lighting hopes that softly sway.
In every turn, a chance awaits,
In this wood where love creates.

Each lingering touch upon the bark,
A whispered wish, a hopeful spark.
As dreams take flight on silver wings,
The magic of the wood still sings.

So let us wander, hand in hand,
In this vast, enchanted land.
With every wish, a journey starts,
In the flourish of our hearts.

Blossoms of Memory in the Ethereal Realm

In the realm where memories drift,
Time unfolds, a precious gift.
Each blossom holds a story dear,
Whispers of laughter, joy, and fear.

Upon the breeze, they twirl and sway,
Carrying fragments of yesterday.
In pink and gold, the petals spread,
A tapestry of words unsaid.

Beneath the stars, the shadows play,
In the hush of night, they softly sway.
Every bloom a journey shared,
In the realm, our hearts laid bare.

Through fragrant fields, we walk as one,
With every step, our fears undone.
In the blossoms, love will gleam,
In this ethereal, endless dream.

Remembered moments bloom anew,
In every shade, in every hue.
In this realm where hearts can soar,
Blossoms of memory, evermore.

Threads of Twilight in the Gossamer Grass

In the dusk where shadows creep,
Whispers cradle secrets deep.
Gossamer threads in twilight weave,
Tales of dreams that we believe.

Softly sighs the evening breeze,
Rustling through the swaying trees.
Stars awaken, twinkling bright,
Guiding hearts into the night.

Moonlight dances on the dew,
Painting skies in shades of blue.
Every blade holds stories old,
Underneath the cosmic fold.

As twilight threads the fabric tight,
Mingling darkness with the light,
Luna's spell wraps round the grass,
In the twilight, moments pass.

Softly now, let dreams entwine,
In this place where starlight shines.
Caught in time's gentle embrace,
In the hush, we find our place.

Dreamscapes of the Ethereal Glade

In the heart where silence hums,
Ethereal light softly comes.
Dreamscapes dwell beneath the trees,
Carried forth on whispered breeze.

Mossy carpets cradle feet,
Where the sun and shadows meet.
Fairy wings and laughter blend,
In this glade, where dreams descend.

Time drifts like the gentle mist,
Every moment feels like bliss.
With starlit eyes, we drift away,
In this magic, here we stay.

Colors swirl, the world ignites,
Painting life with pure delights.
In the glade, the heart takes flight,
Lost in hues of day and night.

Let us dance on dream's sweet shore,
In the glade, forevermore.
Through the twilight, shadows play,
In this world, we find our way.

Twilight's Embrace in the Hidden Hollow

In a hollow wrapped in shade,
Twilight's secrets gently laid.
Crickets sing their evening songs,
Echoes weaving, life belongs.

Beneath the boughs, the whispers call,
Soft like dreams, they rise and fall.
Where the fireflies softly gleam,
In the dark, they paint a dream.

Shadows linger, bathed in gold,
Every corner holds stories old.
In the night's embrace we find,
A sense of wonder intertwined.

As the stars spin tales above,
In this hollow, warm with love.
Magic swirls in every glance,
Guided by the moon's soft dance.

When dawn breaks, our hearts will know,
In the twilight's gentle glow,
Memories wrapped in the night,
Will forever hold us tight.

Veils of Enchantment in the Mist

In the veil of morning mist,
Secrets linger, yet are missed.
Hazy whispers grace the air,
Calling forth a dreamer's dare.

Softly draped in silver threads,
Nature's tapestry spreads.
Every droplet tells a tale,
Hidden paths where wonders sail.

Fog embraces woodland's grace,
Softening each familiar space.
In the stillness, echoes swell,
As unreal as a whispered spell.

Through the gloom, the sunlight fights,
Chasing shadows, igniting sights.
In the blur, we find delight,
Unearthing magic, pure and bright.

As the mist begins to fade,
Stories woven, dreams are made.
In this dance of light and shade,
Veils of wonder never trade.

Twilight Serenade in the Whispering Woods

In twilight's glow, the shadows play,
Soft whispers drift, as night eats day.
Beneath the boughs where secrets lie,
The stars awake in a velvet sky.

Crickets sing their evening tune,
The silver moon, the watchful rune.
With every breath, the magic grows,
In ancient woods where wonder flows.

A brook serenades the age-old trees,
While fireflies dance on the gentle breeze.
Their glimmering light paints fleeting dreams,
In twilight's arms, nothing's as it seems.

The air is thick with stories told,
Of hearts entwined and treasures bold.
A longing gaze, a tender sigh,
In twilight's grasp, we learn to fly.

So linger here, in this sacred space,
Where time stands still, and shadows grace.
Each whispered thought and fading sigh,
A twilight serenade, you can't deny.

Enchantment's Embrace in the Dusky Dell

In dusky dell, where shadows twine,
The air is thick with spell and sign.
Moonbeams dance on the dewy ground,
In magic's clutch, the world's unbound.

Soft murmurs float on the midnight air,
With every glance, a secret shared.
Glowing embers in the night sky gleam,
As starlit pathways weave through a dream.

Cloaked figures glide through foliage dense,
In whispers soft, they weave pretense.
Each rustling leaf tells tales of yore,
In enchantment's grip, we seek for more.

A flicker of light, a ghostly hue,
Inviting hearts to dance anew.
Within each shadow, possibilities bloom,
In dusky dell, love finds its room.

So hold my hand, let's wander wide,
Where magic swells with every stride.
In the dusky dell, lose track of time,
In enchantment's embrace, our spirits climb.

Lush Reveries of an Arcane Hollow

In arcane hollow, where dreams converge,
Lush reveries flow, like a gentle surge.
Mossy banks cradle thoughts so bright,
In emerald shade, we bathe in light.

Ancient thickets, secrets kept,
In whispered breeze, the forest wept.
With every sigh, the air ignites,
As visions bloom in starry nights.

Bubbles of laughter ride the stream,
Where sunlight drapes a golden seam.
And every flower, in colors bold,
Holds tales of magic waiting to unfold.

Time wanders slow in this mystic glade,
Where woven paths of fortune wade.
With every heartbeat, a new delight,
In lush reveries, we take to flight.

So come, dear friend, let's weave our fate,
In arcane hollow, it's never too late.
With hearts unbound, let's chase the stars,
In dreams' embrace, the world is ours.

Silvery Echoes Through the Forgotten Thicket

In forgotten thicket, shadows roam,
Silvery echoes call us home.
With every step, the past aligns,
In moonlight's hue, the magic shines.

Secrets linger in whispered threads,
Where ancient paths weave where hope treads.
Each rustling leaf, a voice of the past,
In silvery whispers, memories cast.

Branch and vine, a tapestry spun,
In twilight hours, all hearts are one.
A fleeting gaze, the night unfurls,
In forgotten thicket, a world of pearls.

Through tangled roots and mossy stone,
We search for truths we've yet to own.
Each echo sings of forgotten lore,
In shadows deep, we seek for more.

Hold tight your courage, let worries sway,
In silvery echoes, we find our way.
For every path, a tale to tell,
In forgotten thicket, all is well.

Enigma of the Shimmering Hollow

In a hollow where whispers twine,
Moonlight dances on the brine.
Shadows flicker, secrets wane,
Echoes of laughter, sweet and plain.

A glimmer found in twilight's lace,
Mysteries swirl in a soft embrace.
Footsteps follow a winding thread,
In the heart of magic, softly tread.

Beneath the boughs, the dreams alight,
Stories merge in the velvet night.
With every heartbeat, a tale unfolds,
In the shimmering hollow, bravery holds.

Night's gentle sigh beckons near,
The shimmer calls; will you adhere?
With each breath, enchantment grows,
In the hollow where the mystery flows.

Dare to glimpse its hidden charms,
Where silence speaks and nature warms.
Enigma lies in the fading glow,
In the shimmering hollow, it whispers low.

Reflections of Forgotten Realms

In realms where time has lost its way,
Mirrors chant of bright decay.
Faded crowns of kings now rust,
In whispers soft, lies ancient trust.

Between the trees, the echoes call,
From hidden realms where shadows fall.
Tales of glory, lost and worn,
In twilight hours, dimly born.

Glimmers of history in mirrored sights,
Glances cast on blighted nights.
Forgotten lands with stories old,
In reflective pools, their dreams unfold.

Curious hearts may dare to see,
The flicker's dance of what could be.
In enchanting sights, lost realms sway,
Whispered promises that fade away.

Dive deep into the echo's light,
Find the secrets hidden from sight.
Reflections hold what time withstood,
In forgotten realms, where dreams once stood.

Dappled Light in an Ethereal Glimpse

Through a forest bathed in gold,
Dappled light weaves tales untold.
Luminous flickers kiss the leaves,
In nature's grasp, the heart believes.

Whispers of fairies softly weave,
Magic stirs in light reprieve.
Fleeting shadows dance and play,
Within the trees, where dreams delay.

Glimmers splashed on misty air,
Moments caught in twilight's snare.
Paths of wonder beckon clear,
In dappled echoes, dreams come near.

Nature paints in colors bright,
Dancing softly in the night.
Each sunbeam blossoms, wild and free,
In an ethereal glimpse, come see.

The forest hums with secrets sly,
As shimmering light begins to sigh.
Intertwined, the ethereal twine,
In dappled beauty, souls align.

The Haunting Song of the Celestial Glen

In the glen where stars descend,
A haunting song begins to blend.
Echoes rise from twilight's veil,
Secrets born in a wispy trail.

Moonlit shadows softly hum,
Ancient melodies that will come.
Cascading notes through misty air,
Melancholy tunes, dreams laid bare.

Whispers tremble with each refrain,
In the glen, where spirits reign.
Softly floating on the breeze,
The song entwined among the trees.

Casting tales of loves once lost,
The haunting echoes count the cost.
In every note, a tear may dwell,
In the celestial glen, hearts swell.

Listen close, the night will teach,
The secrets beneath its gentle reach.
In the glen, where shadows flow,
A haunting song forever glows.

Veils of Illusion in the Fabled Glade

Whispers dance through trees so tall,
Veils of mist at twilight's call.
Shadows flicker, secrets weave,
In a glade where dreamers believe.

Moonlight casts a silver thread,
Guiding hearts where few have tread.
Echoes of laughter, faint yet near,
In the glade, all dreams appear.

Petals flutter, soft and light,
Glowing softly in the night.
Phantoms bloom in the twilight's hush,
In the glade where wishes rush.

Brushing leaves with gilded hands,
A symphony of nature stands.
Here, the past and present blend,
In the fable, where dreams descend.

Enchantments weave like threads divine,
In this glade where starlight shines.
Veils of truth and dreams unfold,
A tale of magic yet untold.

Beneath the Canopy of Celestial Bloom

Beneath the boughs of ancient trees,
Where starlight drips like honeyed breeze.
Petals whisper secrets low,
In a world where wonders glow.

Dreams entwined with silver vines,
Nature's canvas, where fate aligns.
Sunbeams scatter through the leaves,
Nurturing hopes the heart receives.

A symphony of colors bright,
Cascades of joy in fading light.
Time dances, swirling, warm and free,
In the bloom of eternity.

Glimmers flicker, shy and bold,
Stories waiting to be told.
Beneath this sky of endless hue,
Hearts find solace, pure and true.

In every breath, a magic sighs,
Where dreams are born, where magic lies.
Celestial wonders, soft and bright,
Beneath the stars, we find our light.

Enigmatic Journeys through Woven Woods

In woven woods, the shadows play,
A labyrinth where wanderers stray.
Each twisted path, a story spun,
A timeless tale, where all begun.

Leaves of emerald spark with grace,
Embracing secrets in their embrace.
Footsteps echo on the ground,
In this world where dreams are found.

Veils of silence cloak the air,
Murmurs of magic everywhere.
With every turn, a story glows,
In every hesitated prose.

Branches arch like outstretched arms,
Guardians of untold charms.
Through the twilight, we unearth,
The mysteries of life and birth.

Endless journeys await the brave,
In the woods, our dreams we save.
Every whisper, every sigh,
An invitation to the sky.

The Allure of Lost Enclaves

Hidden realms call from afar,
Echoes drifting like a star.
In lost enclaves, shadows twine,
Lessons etched in ancient pine.

Winds of fate swirl through the glade,
Whirling hopes that never fade.
Forgotten paths of yesteryear,
In memory's grasp, we hold them dear.

Mysteries wrapped in twilight's cloak,
Magic sings through every oak.
Within these woods, our dreams awaken,
In the silence, hearts unshaken.

A tapestry of time and space,
We wander through this sacred place.
In every shadow, a truth appears,
Awakening ancient dreams and fears.

In the embrace of dusk's soft glide,
Lost enclaves, where we confide.
Paths forgotten, and tales untold,
In the allure, our souls behold.

Sacred Grounds of the Arcane Grove

In shadows cast by ancient trees,
Where whispers dance upon the breeze,
The echoes of forgotten lore,
Ring softly through the grove once more.

With mossy stones that hum with power,
And blooms that glow with twilight's hour,
A magic old as time holds sway,
In every leaf, in every ray.

To tread upon this hallowed ground,
Is to hear the secrets all around,
Of spirits resting, still and deep,
In dreams of old, where memories sleep.

The moths, they flutter, pale and bright,
Guided by the gentle light,
Of fireflies that weave through night,
And fill the heart with pure delight.

In the Arcane Grove, the world feels whole,
Each whispering rustle soothes the soul,
For here, the magic weaves and spins,
A tapestry, where life begins.

In the Grasp of the Wandering Spirit

Beneath the boughs where shadows play,
A spirit wanders night and day,
In dreams of lost and ancient time,
Its whispers soft, a haunting rhyme.

In every sigh, a tale unfolds,
Of heartbeats fierce and spirits bold,
With glowing eyes that pierce the dark,
And lead the timid to the spark.

To feel its grasp, the cool caress,
Is to be lost, yet feel the bless,
Of magic swirling all around,
In every sigh, in every sound.

Oh, wandering spirit, roam so free,
In moonbeams bright, let us both see,
The paths that twist and turn away,
To stories of another day.

In the grasp of this ethereal friend,
Life's mysteries slowly shall mend,
For in the night's enchanting hold,
New tales arise, both brave and bold.

Wistful Reflections over the Soaring Canopy

Upon the heights where eagles soar,
The world below is rich with lore,
In whispers rustling through the leaves,
The canopy, where time believes.

With twilight hues brushed soft and warm,
And shadows weaving through the charm,
Each sigh of wind a gentle plea,
For dreams that dance in harmony.

Stars twinkle bright in velvet skies,
A tapestry where wonder lies,
Through branches thick, the moonlight spills,
And bathes the earth in tranquil thrills.

Oh, wistful heart, what do you seek?
In nature's arms, the soul can speak,
With every breath, the past ignites,
In soaring dreams through starry nights.

So let us climb these heights above,
And search the stars for tales of love,
For in this lush and lofty place,
We'll find the magic we embrace.

The Hidden Heart of Arcane Dreams

In twilight's hush, where dreams take flight,
A hidden heart beats soft and light,
With secrets held in every shade,
The arcane paths where hope is laid.

Through tangled roots, the stories weave,
Of ancient magic we believe,
Each pulse a promise yet to show,
Amidst the stars, in cosmic flow.

The spirits whisper, soft and low,
In hidden realms where shadows grow,
With every twinkle, every sigh,
The heart reveals what's drawn nigh.

In dreams, we wander, hand in hand,
Through realms of light, a mystic land,
Where hopes alight on wings of fate,
And love endures, a timeless state.

So close your eyes and drift away,
In arcane dreams, let spirit play,
For in the heart, the magic gleams,
A wondrous world of whispered dreams.

Gilded Fragments of a Dreamer's Nest

In twilight's glow, the dreams take flight,
Whispers of wishes, born in the night.
A nest of hope, where glimmers reside,
Fragments of magic, dreams intertwined.

Golden feathers drift on the breeze,
Carried by starlight, soft as a tease.
Each shimmer holds tales of what could be,
In the heart of a dreamer, wild and free.

Soft echoes linger, secrets unfold,
In the embrace of night, stories are told.
Where shadows and memories weave a thread,
Gilded fragments nurture hopes unsaid.

Beneath the moon's eye, thoughts twirl and spin,
A canvas of reveries, life's gentle din.
Each moment a treasure, cherished and bright,
In the dreamer's nest, all hearts take flight.

So gather the dreams that shimmer and gleam,
In the gilded fragments of a fading dream.
Let the magic linger, soft as a sigh,
In the nest of a dreamer, where wishes can fly.

Ethereal Moments in the Garden of Secrets

In the heart of the garden, secrets bloom,
Petals of silence, dispelling the gloom.
Whispers of wonder, soft and serene,
Ethereal moments, where few have been.

Moonlight dances on leaves, a soft glow,
Guiding the dreamers where wild breezes blow.
A tapestry woven with shadows and light,
In the garden of secrets, all feels so right.

Branches entwine, a delicate lace,
Nature's own mementos, a warm embrace.
As dusk falls gently, enchantments arise,
In this hidden realm, beneath starry skies.

Every leaf holds a story, every breeze sings,
A symphony crafted from ephemeral things.
In the heart of the night, where dreams softly tread,
Ethereal moments, where hopes are fed.

The stillness invites you to wander, explore,
In the garden of secrets, forevermore.
Where time stands still, and the magic unfolds,
In moments ethereal, the heart's truth beholds.

Shadows that Dance in Silent Woods

In silent woods, where shadows reside,
Mysteries linger, in whispers they hide.
With each gentle rustle, a tale is spun,
Shadows that dance as the day is done.

Moonbeams peek through the arching trees,
Caressing the forest with soft, tender cheese.
A ballet of spirits in twilight's embrace,
Each movement a story, a timeless grace.

Footfalls are echoes of ages long past,
In the silence, the magic holds fast.
Every flicker of light, a chance to behold,
The secrets of woods where the wild tales unfold.

Veils of the night wrap the trees in their shroud,
Where shadows enchant, and the stillness is loud.
With the pulse of the twilight, the world holds its breath,
In shadows that dance, life whispers of death.

So wander these woods with a heart open wide,
And listen for stories the shadows confide.
In the cradle of night, the enchantment is free,
Shadows that dance beneath the old tree.

Resplendent Whispers in an Ancient Refuge

In an ancient refuge, where echoes are clear,
Resplendent whispers beckon those near.
Time whispers softly through windswept stone,
In secrets of ages, not meant to be known.

The air is thick with the sighs of the past,
Each corner a story, a shadow cast.
Where the sunlight dapples through leafy embrace,
In the warmth of the refuge, find your place.

Through corridors winding like dreams in a haze,
Adventures await in the fading day's gaze.
A tapestry woven from laughter and tears,
Resplendent whispers draw out long-lost fears.

And in every nook where the light softly lands,
The touch of a spirit, the warmth of their hands.
In the silence, the refuge, alight with the glow,
Holds tales of the heart, both high and low.

Take heed of the whispers that drift on the breeze,
For in this old refuge, your heart finds its ease.
Resplendent they shine, bright moments of old,
In the arms of the ancient, true treasures unfold.

Serendipity Found in the Glimmering Mist

In the morn when shadows creep,
A soft embrace, secrets keep.
Glimmers speak of paths unseen,
In the mist, where dreams convene.

Footsteps light on dew-kissed grass,
Twinkling tales that time won't pass.
Every whisper, every hue,
Speaks of wonders, fresh and new.

A fleeting glance, a lingering thought,
In the silence, magic wrought.
Serendipity dances near,
In the heart where hope appears.

Moments woven, fate entwined,
With every breath, the stars aligned.
Through the haze, a truth profound,
In the glimmer, joy is found.

Hope awakens with the dawn,
In the mist, we are reborn.
A tapestry of light is spun,
In serendipity, we run.

Echoes from the Realm of the Enchanted

In the glade where shadows play,
Echoes whisper, night and day.
A melody that calls the brave,
Through the woods, the heart will save.

Mystic voices, gentle sighs,
Beneath the veil of starry skies.
Every note, a tale long lost,
In the magic, we pay the cost.

Fables of the moonlit breeze,
Carried gently, like the trees.
In the silence, secrets share,
From the depths of whispered air.

Through the mist, enchantments rise,
Igniting dreams in eager eyes.
Every heartbeat, every tone,
Reminds us we are not alone.

With every echo, we find light,
In the darkness, sparks ignite.
Realm of wonders, here we stand,
Drawn together, hand in hand.

Tapestry of Whispers in the Midnight Vale

In the vale where shadows wove,
A tapestry of tales so rove.
Whispers dance in moonlit glow,
Secrets flow like streams below.

Starlit threads in night's embrace,
Each woven story finds its place.
With every sigh, a dream takes flight,
In the stillness of the night.

Echoes linger, soft and sweet,
Rooted deep in time's own beat.
Silken strands of laughter weave,
While the midnight spirits cleave.

Through the fog, a glance we share,
In this vale, beyond all care.
Every whisper, chance to see,
The beauty in what's meant to be.

Within this world, we find our song,
A melody where we belong.
In the whispers, hearts unveil,
Tales entwined in the midnight vale.

Celestial Lullabies Beneath the Dancing Light

Underneath the twinkling stars,
Celestial notes from near and far.
A lullaby that softly sways,
Guiding dreams through starry bays.

In the night where wishes twine,
Dancing light, a spark divine.
Every sigh, a heart's embrace,
In the cosmos, we find grace.

Rhythms pulse in quiet air,
Melodies that take us there.
Through the silence, stars ignite,
Waltzing 'neath the cloak of night.

Softly strumming, time moves slow,
With every heartbeat, dreams will grow.
Celestial lullabies unfold,
In whispered tales of love retold.

In the glow of dawn's first light,
As shadows fade, we feel the bright.
With every song beneath the skies,
In harmony, our spirits rise.

Lyricism of the Wandering Breeze

Through silver leaves the whispers flow,
A melody that none can know.
It dances soft through ancient trees,
And carries tales upon the breeze.

The twilight sings of worlds untold,
As starlit secrets dare unfold.
A gentle hum in twilight's grace,
Awakens dreams in nature's embrace.

With every gust, a story spun,
Of laughter shared and shadows run.
In every twist, a breath of life,
A fleeting touch, a hint of strife.

The wandering breeze with tender care,
Brings forth the love that lingers there.
It calls to hearts, both young and wise,
To chase the light beneath the skies.

Within its song, a timeless spark,
Illuminating paths so dark.
For in its flight, we find our way,
As dreams take wing at break of day.

Ornate Veils of the Dreaming Vale

In veils of mist, the dawn awakes,
With whispers soft, the silence breaks.
Where shadows weave the light of day,
A hidden path will guide the way.

The flowers bloom with jeweled grace,
In colors bright, a warm embrace.
They dance beneath the sun's soft gaze,
And paint the vale with golden rays.

As sparkling streams weave tales so old,
Of mysteries in waters cold.
Each ripple sings of joys and fears,
And echoes back through countless years.

The trees, they stand as silent guards,
Of wishes whispered, dreams and shards.
Their leaves like pages, turning slow,
In stories that the breezes know.

In this serene, enchanted place,
Where time and magic intertwine,
The vale invites both soul and mind,
To wander forth, their fate to find.

Song of the Nightingale in the Spellbound Hollow

In hollowed dark, a nightingale,
Sings soft sweet notes, through wood and vale.
Her voice, like silk on velvet air,
A spell is cast; a magic rare.

With every note, the shadows sway,
As stars peek down to hear her play.
The moonlight drapes her in a shroud,
A guardian for the dreaming crowd.

In echoes rich, her song unfolds,
Of love and loss, of dreams retold.
A lullaby for hearts that yearn,
In every note, the embers burn.

Through tangled roots and gleaming streams,
She weaves a path through threaded dreams.
A memory of whispers sweet,
Where hope and sorrow gently meet.

Oh, nightingale, your song shall be,
A balm for souls, a symphony.
In hollowed ground, you raise the dawn,
With every note, a life reborn.

Whispers of Mirth in the Sun-dappled Shadows

In sunlit glades, where laughter lingers,
The shadows dance with playful fingers.
Each beam of light, a joyous chase,
In this realm of sparkling grace.

Beneath the boughs, the secrets bloom,
Of friendship shared in nature's room.
The echoes ring with cheerful glee,
As whispers weave through every tree.

With flowers bright, like gems adorned,
The spirit of the vale is born.
Their colors burst with every sigh,
Inviting all who wander by.

In every breeze, a tale is spun,
Of spirits frolic 'neath the sun.
They twirl and leap, in shadows cast,
Creating memories that hold fast.

So come, dear friend, to join the fray,
In sun-dappled dusk, we'll laugh and play.
For in these moments, rich and true,
The whispers of mirth will dance with you.

Serenity Found in the Nook of Mystery

In a quiet corner, shadows play,
Where every whisper holds a sway.
A twinkling star above does blink,
In the stillness, thoughts do link.

Mossy stones guard stories told,
Of dreams once forged, and realms of old.
The gentle breeze tells tales so sweet,
As nature's heart finds its beat.

Flickering fireflies dance at night,
Painting the air with tiny light.
Embers of calm in twilight's haze,
Wrap the world in tender ways.

Here in the nook, time drifts away,
With every sigh at the end of day.
The secrets kept within the trees,
Whisper of magic in the breeze.

Timeless Wilds of the Whispered Lore

In tangled thickets, stories weave,
Of ancient nights that never cleave.
A melody hums through the leaves,
Of lingering echoes that time retrieves.

Elusive glimmers, laughter's ghost,
Wander through pastures, fair and close.
The sunlight filters, warm and bright,
And dreams take wing in the fading light.

Each blade of grass, a witness to years,
Washed in the rains, blessed by the tears.
A harmony sung by creatures small,
Resounds in the forest, bonding all.

Timeless wilds, where spirits dwell,
Guarding the tales only trees can tell.
In every shadow, the stories sigh,
Alive in the heart, never to die.

Mysteries Hidden in the Swaying Reeds

By the whispering brook, reeds do sway,
Guardians of secrets, night and day.
Each ripple speaks of dreams unseen,
Of wanderers lost, in fields of green.

Footprints faded by the glinting tide,
Lead to a world where spirits glide.
Echoes of laughter, soft and low,
Dance with the wind, the stories flow.

A rustling hush beneath the moon,
Invites the heart to hum a tune.
Time cradles each moment so dear,
In the sway of the reeds, it is here.

Mysteries hidden, forever bound,
In nature's arms, true solace found.
With every ebb and flow of life,
Whispers of peace dissolve all strife.

Silence of the Lavender Grove

In a field adorned with violet haze,
Silence swathes the sun's soft rays.
Each bloom a secret, fragrant and rare,
Breathes in the calm, fills the air.

Gentle hums of bees abide,
While sunbeams drift and shadows glide.
Moments linger as worries fade,
Within this grove, tranquility laid.

A path of gravel, winding slow,
Leads to the heart of lavender's glow.
The world beyond seems far away,
In this haven, where spirits play.

Silence reigns in royal tones,
Where peace unfolds and love condones.
In every petal, stories bloom,
In the lavender grove, cease the gloom.

Secrets Spun in Serpentine Shadows

In darkness deep, where whispers dwell,
A tale entwined, no words to tell.
With shadows cast and secrets spun,
The serpent's dance has just begun.

Beneath the moon's soft silver light,
A world of dreams takes silent flight.
The echoes beckon, calling near,
To those who listen, without fear.

Among the trees, the spirits sigh,
In tangled roots where phantoms lie.
Each winding path, a hidden lore,
Unlocks the heart forevermore.

The mist will rise, the veil will thin,
Revealing truths held deep within.
For every secret, a choice must fall,
In serpentine shadows, heed the call.

So venture forth, let wonder gleam,
Embrace the magic, follow the dream.
With courage bound, let shadows part,
For secrets spun will light the heart.

Whispering Leaves of the Arcane Hollow

In Arcane Hollow, leaves do weave,
A tapestry of dreams to believe.
With every rustle, mysteries grow,
As ancient tales begin to flow.

Beneath the boughs, soft voices play,
They tell of night and glide away.
The whispers brush against the skin,
Inviting souls to journey in.

Where sunlight dances on the ground,
The secrets of the woods abound.
Each leaf a keeper, each breeze a guide,
Through enchanted realms where wonders hide.

The essence of the earth, so pure,
Holds magic close, in roots and fir.
A sacred place where spirits dwell,
In whispering leaves, all is well.

So listen closely, hear the call,
Let visions rise and shadows fall.
For in this hollow, life anew,
Awaits the seeker brave and true.

Twilight's Tapestry in the Lush Embers

Beneath the veil of twilight's grace,
Lush embers glow in soft embrace.
The colors merge, a dance so rare,
As night unveils its mystic snare.

With fireflies kindling starlit dreams,
The world transforms with silver beams.
Each whisper winds through dusky air,
Creating magic, raw and rare.

In glades adorned with shadowed light,
Nature's pulse ignites the night.
Each flicker speaks, each spark ignites,
A tapestry of lost delights.

The sky is cloaked in velvet deep,
As secrets spun in silence keep.
With every breath, the night descends,
In twilight's arms, the heart transcends.

So wander forth where dreams reside,
Let lush embers be your guide.
For in this glow, the heart will see,
The endless dance of mystery.

Mysterious Murmurs Among the Ferns

Amidst the ferns, a soft refrain,
Mysterious murmurs linger, remain.
Each leafy frond, a tale to share,
Of secrets spun in whispered air.

In tangled green, where shadows play,
Ancient spirits softly sway.
They hum of ages, lost in time,
Each note a story, pure and prime.

The dew-kissed leaves, like jewels bright,
Hold echoes of the long-lost night.
Their rhythms hark to nature's song,
A dance of memories, vast and strong.

With every step through emerald glades,
The heart awakens, gently swayed.
For in the hush, the world will turn,
And from the ferns, new wonders burn.

So lean in close, hear nature's call,
Let murmurs rise, let spirits enthrall.
For in the ferns, with grace and might,
Life's mystery glimmers, pure and bright.

Whispers of Enchanted Fields

In fields where shadows gently creep,
The whispers of the night take sweep.
With flowers dancing in the light,
Their colors fade away from sight.

A breeze that carries tales of old,
Of faeries, dreams, and hearts so bold.
The crickets sing a lullaby,
As silver stars adorn the sky.

The moon casts soft its tranquil rays,
Illuminating hidden ways.
Each step a secret, soft and slight,
In enchanted fields of endless night.

Where time stands still and wonders grow,
The magic flows, a gentle flow.
With every sigh and every glance,
The world around begins to dance.

Here in the depths of twilight's charm,
The softest spell still holds its arm.
In whispers, dreams begin to weave,
In fields where none would dare believe.

Moonlit Dews on Mystic Meadows

Beneath the gaze of silver moons,
The meadow sways to nature's tunes.
With dewdrops glistening like stars,
The night unfolds its hidden bars.

Each blade of grass a shimmering gem,
Reflecting light in nature's realm.
The whispers of the nightingale,
In moonlit magic, tell their tale.

Silent breezes weave through the night,
Caressing dreams with soft delight.
As shadows dance beneath the trees,
The world knows peace with gentle ease.

With every breath, a secret sigh,
In moonlit dews, the memories lie.
The mystic meadows hold their grace,
In every glimmer, find your place.

In twilight's arms, the echoes call,
For those who wander, come, enthrall.
Through moonlit paths where wishes flow,
In mystic meadows, heartbeats glow.

Secrets of the Sylvan Expanse

In sylvan realms where shadows play,
Secrets whisper through the day.
Among the trees so tall and wise,
Ancient magic softly lies.

With every leaf that flutters past,
The echoes of the ages cast.
Here where the sunbeams weave a spell,
In every corner secrets dwell.

The winding paths of mossy green,
Lead to wonders yet unseen.
The brook that babbles, tales to share,
Of spirits dancing in the air.

In twilight's glow, the sprites emerge,
From shadows deep, they start to surge.
With laughter ringing, hearts entwine,
In sylvan expanse, all is divine.

So wander deep where few have trod,
Embrace the magic, feel the nod.
The trees will guide you, sweet and clear,
To secrets held within our sphere.

Shadows Beneath the Whispering Leaves

Beneath the leaves, shadows entwine,
In whispers soft, the secrets shine.
Each gust of wind a tale retold,
Of days gone by and dreams of old.

The rustle plays a haunting tune,
As twilight paints the world with rune.
In hidden nooks, the fairies peep,
While twilight's watch lulls all to sleep.

In silence, every heart can hear,
The magic that whispers near.
In every curl of misty air,
Lies centuries of love and care.

The dance of shadows, soft and light,
In whispers deep, invites the night.
For those who pause to seek and see,
The beauty held in mystery.

So linger long where night befalls,
And hear the whispers in the thralls.
For shadows tell of dreams believed,
Beneath the leaves, all souls retrieved.

Mystic Glades of Enchanted Mists

In the glades where whispers dwell,
Mists weave tales, of magic spell.
The moonlight dances on the streams,
Caressing dreams, igniting seams.

Fairies flit on silken wings,
With laughter soft, the echo rings.
Beneath the boughs, secrets lay,
In the quiet of the day.

Ancient trees with bark of gold,
Hold the stories yet untold.
The shadows play with fleeting light,
In the heart of endless night.

A whispered breeze through leaves will flow,
Guiding hearts where wonders grow.
In the glade, a truth will bloom,
This enchanted world's sweet perfume.

So wander forth, let spirits lead,
To where the heart finds all it needs.
In mystic glades, the soul will soar,
Forever seeking, ever more.

Secrets Whispered in the Moonlit Grove

In the grove where shadows sigh,
Secrets weave 'neath silver sky.
The nightingale sings soft and clear,
To charm the stars, to quell the fear.

Twilight's veil with magic spun,
Hides the tales of all that's done.
Whispers echo, soft and frail,
As twilight tells a secret tale.

Beneath the branches interlaced,
Stories of old are gently traced.
With each rustle, a promise made,
In the heart of the glimmering glade.

Night blooms fresh like tender rose,
With twinkling lights that freely chose.
To cloak the past in gentle mist,
In the grove where dreams exist.

So linger long, let time unfurl,
In the moonlit world, let hearts whirl.
For every secret softly shared,
Weaves a bond that's always cared.

Gossamer Dreams of the Hidden Vale

In a vale where shadows play,
Gossamer dreams drift and sway.
Velvet petals on the ground,
In silence, beauty can be found.

Whispers ride the gentle breeze,
Carried forth through ancient trees.
Where echoing footsteps softly tread,
And woven tales are gently spread.

A shimmering mist, a fairy's sigh,
Calls the wanderer to fly high.
On feathery thoughts, so light, so free,
In the vale, just you and me.

Stars above begin to gleam,
Reflecting hopes that gently stream.
As night enfolds the world so small,
The hidden vale can hold it all.

So chase the dreams that twinkle bright,
Let shadows blend with dawning light.
In gossamer threads, love will weave,
A tapestry that none can leave.

Shadows of the Ethereal Path

Upon the path where shadows play,
The ethereal light begins to sway.
Footsteps echo with gentle grace,
As whispers linger in this space.

Moonbeams dance on cobblestones,
Where every heart can find its home.
Each stone a memory, softly laid,
In the twilight's tender shade.

The wind carries a haunting tune,
That swirls like dust beneath the moon.
With every change of night's embrace,
A story weaves in time and place.

So walk with courage, brave and true,
Through shadows deep, a path anew.
For magic beckons in the dark,
As fires whisper, leaving marks.

In ethereal realms, let spirits soar,
With every stride, discover more.
The shadows dance, the night will sing,
To hearts awakened, life will bring.

Fantasies Unraveled in the Starlit Thicket

In the thicket where shadows play,
Whispers of dreams drift far away.
Stars twinkle like secrets untold,
Looming tales of courage unfold.

Moonlit paths where fairies dance,
In their sway, we find our chance.
Each glimmer weaves a story bright,
In the heart of this enchanted night.

Beneath the boughs, old legends cry,
Stories of love that never die.
Breezes carry the songs of yore,
In these woods, magic's at the core.

With every rustle, a promise grows,
Of hidden worlds the heart now knows.
In the starlit glow, hopes take flight,
Guided by dreams wrapped in light.

A heartbeat echoes in the air,
Inviting us to shed our care.
In the stillness, our spirits blend,
In the thicket, where fantasies mend.

Dappled Light in the Bewitched Vale

In the vale where shadows sleep,
Beneath the willows, secrets keep.
Dappled light through leaves does gleam,
Weaving spells like a waking dream.

Mossy stones and lilies fair,
Nature's wonders hang in the air.
In every petal, magic swirls,
Unfolding tales of ancient worlds.

Whispers float on the gentle breeze,
All around, the heart finds ease.
Here in this realm where spirits roam,
The earth cradles every lost home.

Sunlit pools reflect the sky,
In their depths, lost wishes lie.
Every ripple, an echo of fate,
In this vale, all hearts await.

As dusk descends, colors collide,
In the bewitched, no need to hide.
With each heartbeat, life intertwines,
In nature's grasp, our hope aligns.

Chants of Nature's Arcane Realm

In nature's realm where echoes sing,
Soft whispers of the wild take wing.
Through every branch, a melody flows,
A symphony that only nature knows.

Vibrant hues of green abound,
In each leaf, a story found.
Chants resound from the earth's deep core,
Invoking wisdom from days of yore.

Mist weaves tales in the morning light,
Casting shadows that dance in flight.
The air hums with the promise of grace,
Within this realm, we find our place.

Moonlit nights hold secrets dear,
In their stillness, the heart draws near.
The world spins gently on nature's breath,
In its embrace, we uncover depth.

Each rise of dawn brings forth the chance,
To join the earth in nature's dance.
In sacred trust, we hear the call,
In this arcane realm, we are all.

Fables of Magic in the Verdant Realm

In the verdant woods where wonders bloom,
Magic lingers in every room.
Fables told by the flickering flame,
Whispers of hope in an ancient name.

With tangled vines, the stories weave,
In hushed tones, they urge us to believe.
Every creature with a tale to share,
In this realm, love hangs in the air.

From the brook where the wild things play,
To the skies painted at end of day.
Each drop of dew holds a captured dream,
In the magic, there flows a gleam.

As twilight falls, the stars awaken,
A canopy where dreams are taken.
In the hush, time spins a thread,
Binding all that has been said.

Through fragrant blooms and twilight's sigh,
Fables live on, they never die.
In the heart of the woods, we find our way,
In the verdant realm, where magic stays.

Lullabies of the Bewitched Grove

In a grove where shadows softly sway,
Moonlit whispers drift and play,
Among the trees, a song takes flight,
Lulling the stars to sleep at night.

A gentle breeze with secrets grand,
Carries tales from a distant land,
Where magic blooms in softest hues,
And every heart can chase its muse.

The owls sing low, the fireflies gleam,
In this realm, we weave our dream,
Beneath the branches, wild and free,
Where every spark holds mystery.

As night descends, the world will yawn,
Echoes of enchantment greet the dawn,
In the stillness, let your worries cease,
And nestle deep in twilight's peace.

So hush, dear child, and close your eyes,
Feel the magic as it softly sighs,
For in the grove, where wonders weave,
The lullabies of night believe.

Serpentine Paths through the Enchanted Wilds

Winding trails of ancient trees,
Whispers carried on the breeze,
Hidden secrets, soft and bright,
Lead the way from dark to light.

With every step, a tale unfolds,
Of whispered dreams and secrets told,
Through mossy floors, the fae will twirl,
In the wilds, their joy unfurl.

Glimmers dance upon the brook,
The fairies smile, the creatures look,
Where twilight weaves its mystic map,
Around each curve, in nature's lap.

Starlit skies above us gleam,
As we tread softly, lost in dream,
Each rustling leaf, a soft refrain,
In enchanted wilds, we find no pain.

So come, dear heart, and take my hand,
Together through this wondrous land,
On serpentine paths, we shall roam,
In the wilds, we find our home.

Echoes of Sorcery in the Delicate Breeze

In the hush of twilight's grace,
Sorcery stirs in a gentle space,
Echoes ripple through the air,
Carried softly, like a prayer.

Whispers of old, both faint and clear,
Speak of magic that lingers near,
Each note a charm, each sound a spell,
In the breeze, we hear its swell.

Dancing shadows play on the ground,
With every flicker, enchantments abound,
Let the mysteries draw you close,
For in the wind, the world we host.

Moonbeams fall on the winding paths,
Trickling laughter, magical baths,
As echoes twirl and softly blend,
The sorcery whispers, never to end.

So close your eyes, and feel the sway,
Of enchanting winds that softly play,
For in this moment, you'll find your ease,
In the echoes of sorcery in the breeze.

Glistening Dreams of the Mysterious Glen

In the glen where secrets hide,
Glistening dreams in shadows glide,
Underneath the silver boughs,
Magic flourishes and somehow.

A sparkling brook with laughter flows,
Carving paths where wonder grows,
With every ripple, stories dart,
Splashing tales to warm the heart.

Among the ferns and elder trees,
Whimsies float on evening's breeze,
Creatures, tiny, bright, and shy,
Watch the stars unfold the sky.

Dusk wraps arms around the glen,
As night calls softly, yet again,
In dreams, we wander, wild and free,
Unlocked by whispers, just you and me.

So let the dreams take flight tonight,
In the glen, beneath soft light,
For every heart, a chance to gleam,
In the glistening dreams of a mysterious gleam.

Fables of the Moonlit Meadow

In a meadow where shadows play,
The moon whispers secrets, soft and gray.
Mysterious creatures dance through the night,
Weaving stories in silver light.

Beneath the trees, their branches sway,
Glimmers of starlight lead the way.
Each blade of grass tells a tale,
Of dreams that linger, of wishes pale.

The nightingale sings, a haunting tune,
Echoing softly under the moon.
Laughter of fairies, carried on air,
Fables of magic, beyond compare.

Whispers of lovers who shared a glance,
In the moonlit meadow, lost in a trance.
Their hearts entwined like vines in a kiss,
A fleeting moment, a timeless bliss.

As dawn approaches, the stories fade,
But in every heart, the memories wade.
For magic lingers, though light must reign,
In the moonlit meadow, love shall remain.

Fragrant Echoes of a Timeless Haven

In a haven kissed by blossoms bright,
Fragrances dance on the wings of light.
Petals fall softly, like whispered sighs,
Dreams are born where the beauty lies.

Rivers hum tunes of days long past,
With every ripple, memories cast.
Beneath the boughs where the secrets dwell,
The stories of ages weave their spell.

Sunlight trickles through leaves of green,
Painting the canvas with glimmers serene.
Each breath a fragrance, rich and deep,
Awakening feelings from slumbered sleep.

In the air, hints of jasmine twine,
Stirring the heart with a flavor divine.
Every corner, a world to explore,
In fragrant echoes, forevermore.

With every sunset, the haven glows,
As stars awaken, the magic flows.
Timeless whispers wrap around my soul,
In fragrant echoes, I feel whole.

Musical Breeze of the Wistful Glade

In the glade where the wildflowers sway,
A musical breeze begins to play.
Notes flutter gently on wings of the air,
A symphony built on dreams laid bare.

Each rustling leaf joins the soft refrain,
As memories beckon, like drops of rain.
The brook babbles secrets, old and wise,
Under the gaze of the softening skies.

Scoops of laughter echo from trees,
Mixing with whispers of dancing bees.
All nature joins in the wondrous song,
A melody weaving where we belong.

The twilight glimmers, a beautiful sight,
As shadows extend, embracing the night.
The moon hums along, a lullaby sweet,
In the wistful glade where wonders meet.

In every breeze, a memory twirls,
Carried aloft where the magic unfurls.
Together we sway in laughter and grief,
In the musical breeze, find solace and relief.

Aethereal Hues in the Twilight Realm

In the twilight realm where day meets night,
Aethereal hues dance, a wondrous sight.
Lavenders whisper secrets to gold,
As stories of twilight begin to unfold.

The sky brushes colors against the stars,
Painting the canvas of dreams without bars.
Each shade tells a tale of hope and despair,
In the twilight realm, magic lingers in air.

The hush of the evening, soft like a sigh,
Calls forth the wonders that flutter and fly.
Crickets compose with the wind's gentle breath,
In harmony stitched through the fabric of death.

A world painted gently with whispers and gleam,
Where shadows and light blend in an endless dream.
Each heartbeat resonates with the pulse of the night,
In aethereal hues, where the soul takes flight.

As darkness blankets the happenings dear,
The twilight dances, inviting us near.
Embrace the magic, let your spirit roam,
In the twilight realm, we find our home.

www.ingramcontent.com/pod-product-compliance
Lightning Source LLC
Chambersburg PA
CBHW051943220125
20712CB00003B/96